Discovering
JOBS

Jobs If You Like
VIDEO GAMES

Terri Dougherty

ReferencePoint Press®

San Diego, CA

© 2022 ReferencePoint Press, Inc.
Printed in the United States

For more information, contact:
ReferencePoint Press, Inc.
PO Box 27779
San Diego, CA 92198
www.ReferencePointPress.com

LIBRARY OF CONGRESS CATALOGING-IN-PUBLICATION DATA

Names: Dougherty, Terri, author.
Title: Jobs if you like video games / by Terri Dougherty.
Description: San Diego, CA : ReferencePoint Press, Inc., 2022. | Series:
    Discovering jobs | Includes bibliographical references and index.
Identifiers: LCCN 2021037193 (print) | LCCN 2021037194 (ebook) | ISBN
    9781678202309 (library binding) | ISBN 9781678202316 (ebook)
Subjects: LCSH: Video games industry--Vocational guidance--Juvenile
    literature. | Video games--Design--Vocational guidance--Juvenile
    literature.
Classification: LCC HD9993.E452 D68 2022 (print) | LCC HD9993.E452
    (ebook) | DDC 794.8023--dc23
LC record available at https://lccn.loc.gov/2021037193
LC ebook record available at https://lccn.loc.gov/2021037194

INTRODUCTION: CONNECTING WITH A GROWING INDUSTRY

With nowhere to go during the COVID-19 pandemic, teenager Sophie Keil hunkered down at home with some new friends. She joined millions of others playing *Animal Crossing: New Horizons*, a video game where players create a village on an island and spend their days catching fish, collecting shells, and visiting with talking animal friends. "*Animal Crossing* is so simple and nice," she says. "It's a peaceful game."[1]

The opportunity to take people to different worlds where they can connect and escape is one reason Jeremy Newton loves his career as a video game software engineer. "As a game developer, you're building and sharing something that brings happiness to someone you may never meet,"[2] says Newton, who works for a mobile game company.

A Growing Industry

If you like playing video games, those hours you've spent with your fingers on a keyboard or with a controller in your hands can lead to a career in a growing industry. Video games soared in popularity during the COVID-19 pandemic, as the lockdowns kept people from gathering and forced them to find entertainment at home. Many turned to *Animal Crossing*, *Call of Duty*, *Spider-Man*, *Madden NFL*, *Super Mario 3D All-Stars*, and other video games for fun and virtual companionship. Market intelligence firm IDC estimates that consumers around the world spent $179.7 billion on video games in 2020—20 percent more than in the previous year.

Even before the pandemic hit, the video game industry was on an upswing. Video game spending in the United States almost doubled between 2010 and 2020, from $27 billion to $50 billion, according to market research firm NPD Group.

Mobile, Esports, and More

This growth was powered in part by mobile games like *Candy Crush Saga*, *Pokemon Go*, and *Scribble Rider*, which are easy to download and play on a smartphone. As more people began to use smartphones, more game apps were developed for phones, and the industry rapidly expanded. The growth of mobile games is expected to continue as internet data becomes more affordable around the world, according to a report from researchandmarkets.com.

The rapid growth of esports, where players compete in games such as *Fortnite* and *Counter-Strike*, has also strengthened the video game market. Esports has turned into a billion-dollar industry, as it generates revenue from sponsorships, advertising, and merchandise. Streaming services such as Twitch and YouTube Games also contributed to its rise in popularity, as they allow fans to connect with streamers.

Varied Career Options

A passion for video games might lead to a job as a mobile game developer or esports competitor, but those are far from the only careers that that interest could bring. The industry needs programmers, game testers, artists, composers, voice actors, event planners, announcers, and marketers. Familiarity with game engines, the software used to create a game and make it playable, is a plus in many fields as companies turn to gamification to add interest to websites or online offerings.

Mojan Ahmadi saw this when she logged into her company's insurance portal and saw a gamified option for one of the company's insurance forms. "Getting a degree in game development may open up more job opportunities than you traditionally thought about," said Ahmadi, director of career services at DigiPen Institute of Technology in Redmond, Washington. "At this point the audience is no longer just gamers," she notes. "We are seeing non-game industries wanting game-related knowledge."[3]

Skills developed while playing video games can also help a person thrive in any workplace. Researchers from the Missouri University of Science and Technology found that video game players tend to have attributes like agreeableness, openness, and conscientiousness that can help them succeed as members of workplace teams.

Parents once questioned whether hours spent playing video games could help with their children's job prospects. Those doubts may be gone for good, as the industry is poised for growth and the job outlook remains bright and varied. Video games may be a pastime or hobby for now, but they could reward you with a promising career.

That's Sloane Miller's plan. She grew up playing *Pokémon* and *Minecraft* and is majoring in computer and information sciences with a minor in game modeling and design at North Carolina Agricultural and Technical State University. Hoping for a career as a video game developer, she'd like to create games that help people connect and forge friendships like those she's made playing games like *Overwatch* and *Splatoon 2*. "Video games are more than entertainment," Miller says. "They are a method to connect and showcase our skills and creativity over shared interests."[4]

GAME DESIGNER

What Does a Game Designer Do?

Kelly Toyama has been making games since he was five years old, when he created card and board games on paper. Now a video game designer who has worked on games such as *Assassin's Creed: Bloodlines* and *Age of Empires: Mythologies*, he has turned his childhood interest into a successful career. It's not only his ideas that make the games he works on a success, however. He sees both a love of games and an understanding of collaboration as central to a career as a game designer. "Passion and teamwork are the things that get the job done," he says. "The best games are made when the whole team believes in it and understands the idea. You are the visionary, but that means gathering together the vision of the team."[5]

Game designers oversee the development of a video game or improve an existing game. Designers (sometimes called game directors, design directors, lead designers, or world designers) come up with the unique features that set a game apart from other games. They understand a game's central vision and make sure everyone on the team is working toward bringing that vision to life. A game designer creates a game's theme and features, including characters, situations, and the tools characters use. The designer makes sure that a game flows as expected, that it engages players, immerses them in its world, and makes them want to keep playing.

A game designer leads the team of professionals who specialize in different aspects of the game creation process. This includes other designers, artists, animators, audio engineers, programmers, and quality assurance testers. Designers troubleshoot problems and use feedback and input from team members to make sure the game works as users expect it to. They communicate with team members to keep up with how the project is progressing and to make sure things are working as they should.

Budgets and deadlines are also a game designer's responsibility. The game designer makes sure a game is ready to preview at a gaming conference or for release to customers on time. Ultimately, a game needs to make a profit to be successful, and its designer is also tasked with making sure the cost of developing the game stays within the budgeted amount. The designer may meet with company executives to talk about finances and explain how the amount being spent on the project compares to the amount budgeted for it. If a company decides to reduce the amount of money spent on producing a game, it's the game designer's job to figure out where to make cuts and how to get the game finished for less money.

A Typical Workday

Video game designers tackle a wide range of tasks during the workday. They oversee the production process, making sure the artwork has the right look, that coding is moving along, and that the game's features are working properly. A game designer has to be ready to contribute wherever needed. A designer may create a new feature for a game or find a better way to test software. On smaller teams, designers may need to take on more roles, from programming to testing, while making sure everything stays organized. A designer also needs to be ready to handle unexpected problems. Budgets may be cut, software problems may arise, or

At the Center of It All

"Design is really the go-between with all the disciplines. We have to ride between art, code and production, driving the product forward. It's design's job to try to have a vision of how the game works, what makes it fun, and to be a leader on the team to guide them towards that goal. . . . The best part is the collaboration. Making games is a team sport and being a good designer is about recognizing good ideas, not necessarily having them yourself. Working with a team of talented people to make fun, elegant games is the best part by far."

—Kelly Toyama, video game designer

Quoted in Jason W. Bay, "How to Become a Video Game Designer," Game Industry Career Guide. www.gameindustrycareerguide.com.

the artwork or audio might not be capturing the right tone for the project. The designer needs to think through options and decide how to overcome obstacles.

A designer's workday often involves collaborating and communicating with teammates. As deadlines near, tensions can rise. There may be drama and conflict to address, and the designer needs to work through any issues and make sure the team continues working as a cohesive unit.

Education and Training

Game designers typically have a bachelor's degree in computer programming, game design, or a related field. They must have strong technical knowledge and often study coding. They may also be familiar with the computer programs used in creating graphics and animation. Project management courses are beneficial, as designers oversee a game's production timeline and budget.

Players May Be In for a Surprise

"Playing games and creating games are very different experiences. It's not uncommon for us to see a game enthusiast [who thinks] they know how to make games. Then they see the game creation experience and realize it's incongruent with the game playing experience.

It's a very rigorous field. People think it's lax because games are fun, but it's a lot of hard work to make the game fun for someone else. There are lots of layers to doing what may seem like a very simple action."

—Mojan Ahmadi, director of career services at DigiPen Institute of Technology in Redmond, Washington, interview with the author, May 13, 2021.

Game designers also need to be able to communicate effectively. They must understand how to collaborate with a team and present information. Writing and public speaking classes are beneficial, and working with classmates on projects, games, and other class assignments builds teamwork skills. Because game designers oversee all aspects of a game's creation, they often work in other roles, such as game tester, before being promoted to the game designer role.

Skills and Personality

A game designer needs to be imaginative and creative in order to develop a game's storyline, world, challenges, and puzzles and present them in a way that is entertaining, suspenseful, and challenging. Because game designers are responsible for making sure the finished product is working as it should, they need to see the big picture and understand how the pieces of a game work together to create a fun experience for players. The designer needs to think through how a game's obstacles are overcome and make sure the game's journey and outcome make sense.

At the same time, a game designer must pay attention to a game's details. This quality is so important to Survios, a California-based company that creates virtual reality content, that its game designer job post requires applicants to use the phrase "beauty is in the details" in their cover letter. This assures them that applicants have really read and paid attention to the details of the job description.

To ensure that deadlines are met, game designers need strong organizational skills. They keep track of the progress being made by the game's artists, audio engineers, programmers, and other team members. In addition, they need to be comfortable with communicating and sharing information, as they must keep team members and company executives informed of the game's progress. They provide updates on any changes in the direction of the game's theme or features and also break the news when setbacks occur or glitches need to be fixed.

The workday is often hectic, and many things will be vying for a game designer's attention and time. A designer needs to prioritize, manage time wisely, and understand what to focus on. "To be a video game designer, you have to be ready to do your share of the work quickly and entirely," says Nichole Hall, a student studying game and interactive media design at Rider University in Lawrenceville, New Jersey. "Failing to do your part affects everyone negatively. This is where time management is especially important,"[6] Hall explains.

A game designer needs to have a firm understanding of a game's concept and features, but must also be open-minded. Because of technical or budgetary limitations, some planned features might not work. Designers need to be flexible and ready to incorporate updates and changes into a game when it's called for.

It's inevitable that a project will encounter setbacks. A designer needs be ready to step in, take on challenges, and develop workable solutions. Video game production can be a grueling experience, and a designer needs to have the persistence required to pull it off. "Game design is a tiring, intense job, but also one that is very fulfilling," Hall says. "You have to have the energy and passion to be a game designer, because if you don't, you'll find the work draining."[7]

Working Conditions

Game designers have traditionally worked in an office environment. This allows them to communicate with team members to check on status updates, answer questions, and offer feedback.

Since the COVID-19 pandemic, more opportunities for remote work have opened up. During the pandemic, many employees had to work from home. This forced companies and workers to become more adept at collaborating and communicating virtually. As the pandemic eased, many companies allowed employees to continue working from home every day or several days a week to help workers cut back the time and expense of commuting and help companies save money on office rentals.

While remote work can be an option, the in-office environment of a video game company may offer some fun perks. For example, at the Electronic Arts studio in midtown Sacramento, California, workers have console game competitions and play board games. Coworkers can also get together for weekend adventures.

Video game developers work a forty-hour week and put in overtime when necessary. Game development often includes a period called "crunch mode." When a deadline is looming (perhaps developers are getting a game ready for a conference, or the final release date of the game is near) game designers may need to work fifty, sixty, or even a hundred hours a week.

Employers and Earnings

Game designers may work for large video game companies such as Microsoft, Sony, or Blizzard Entertainment, or they may work at a smaller video game company. Many video game companies are located in California or Texas.

Video game designers make an average of $130,000 per year, according to ZipRecruiter. The salary ranges from $51,000 to $400,000. Most of time the salary is between $76,500 and $130,000.

Future Outlook

The video game industry is growing, and demand for game designers is expected to grow along with it. The Bureau of Labor Statistics includes video game designers in the Special Effects Artists and Animators category and expects jobs to grow by 4 percent by 2029. This is the same as the national average.

Find Out More

Entertainment Software Association

www.theesa.com

This organization advocates for video game creators and companies that publish computer and video games. It provides video game industry news and insights into legal, policy, and public affairs matters.

Game Designing

www.gamedesigning.org

This website provides articles and resources relating to schools and careers for people interested in game design. It also offers information about game engines.

Game Industry Career Guide

www.gameindustrycareerguide.com

This website offers advice on how to get a job in the game industry. It includes information about schools and scholarships, has links to job postings, and features interviews with individuals working in the video game industry.

Gamesindustry.biz

www.gamesindustry.biz

This website offers global news about the video game industry. It also has job postings, articles providing career advice, and information about international events.

PROFESSIONAL GAMER

What Does a Professional Gamer Do?

Arkhram, aka Diego Palma, is soaring and slashing his way through the *Fortnite* landscape. To break down barriers, he expertly flips from one weapon to another and jumps, runs, and glides to his destination. One of the top players in the world, Arkhram won more than $600,000 in tournaments over a span of two years. He broadcasts and archives his gameplay on his Twitch channel, and has more than 190,000 followers.

Professional gamers like Arkhram excel at playing video games. They understand how to navigate a game's challenges, make the right decisions in critical situations, and use strategy to come out on top. They have the skill to compete at a high level.

Professional gamers are entertaining and fun to watch. They make exciting moves and navigate tough situations. As they play they talk with their teammates, breaking down the action or discussing what they've been up to lately. While they're streaming they also keep an eye on the chat, answering questions from viewers and replying to comments.

A Typical Workday

Professional gamers spend much of the day practicing or broadcasting their gameplay. They don't have a typi-

A Few Facts

Typical Earnings
$48,870 annually*

Educational Requirements
No formal education needed, but excellent gaming skills are required

Personal Qualities
Interesting personality, tenaciousness, dedication, focus

Work Settings
Game house, home office

* Average annual pay from ZipRecruiter, 2021

cal 9-to-5 schedule, but do have a structured day. Large blocks of time are set aside for team and individual practice and streaming sessions.

Arkhram works on his *Fortnite* skills ten hours a day. He reviews his games to watch for mistakes and learn strategy, plays the game, and streams on Twitch. "A lot of what we do doesn't come naturally," he said. "We have to prepare, train, analyze, and develop strategies and when you play on a team like I do, you have to collaborate."[8]

Some pro gamers have daytime work hours, but many work in the late afternoon and evening. Lynnie "artStar" Noquez plays *Counter-Strike* with the gaming team Dignitas and describes her day this way:

- 11 a.m. Wake up and reply to work emails.
- Noon to 1 p.m. Get ready for the day and have lunch.
- 1 to 5 p.m. Run errands, clean the house, or spend time with family and friends
- 5 p.m. *Counter-Strike* practice (watching a demo, reviewing play, playing with a pick-up group, streaming on Twitch)
- 7 p.m. Team practice
- Brief mid-practice break for dinner
- 11 p.m. Practice Ends

"I usually head straight to bed and repeat the next day for 5 days a week,"[9] she says.

Until they earn enough money to game full-time, another job might be part of a gamer's schedule. Emmalee "EMUHLEET" Garrido balanced work as a nurse with gaming before turning to gaming full-time. Before becoming a member of the Dignitas team, she would wake up at 4 or 5 a.m., drive to her job in Los Angeles, work for seven or eight hours, make the two-to-three-hour drive home, and then practice gaming. She had to schedule everything—from meals to showers—to make sure she could fit

15

it all in. "I wanted to play with my team so bad I just found this natural energy," she says. "I was so passionate about wanting to be the best and competing."[10]

Education and Training

There are no educational requirements to become a professional gamer. It does, however, require hours of practice and skill at a particular game, such as *Fortnite*, *Call of Duty*, *Counter-Strike*, *Rocket League*, *FIFA*, or *Valorant*. Gamers play the game over and over, learning how to make a move at just the right moment to get the biggest benefits from their actions.

Professional gamers get better by studying recordings of their games. When they're part of a team, they analyze the game with their teammates so they can do a better job of working together.

Pros sharpen their skills by playing against team members or logging onto a game being played online. Teams also scrimmage against each other as they prepare to compete in esports tournaments.

When She Knew

"I will never forget this: the moment we were walking on that stage was kind of like in the movies where time just freezes. That was a euphoric moment. I slowly looked to my left, and I saw my teammates, looked to my right and I saw our coach, and then looked out to the crowd where everyone was cheering under the lights. That was the moment when I knew this was something that I wanted to do for a very long time."

—Professional gamer Emmalee "EMUHLEET" Garrido, describing playing in the Grand Finals at her first international competition, the Electronic Sports World Cup in Paris.

Bence Loksa, "How To Be a Nurse and a Female Pro Gamer at the Same Time—An Interview with Emmalee 'EMUHLEET' Garrido," ESTNN, June 12, 2021. https://estnn.com.

Professional gamers spend hours practicing games, either on their own or with teammates. This helps them learn to make the right moves at the right moments for the biggest gain.

Skills and Personality

A professional gamer must be incredibly skilled at playing a video game. Quick reflexes and finger dexterity are needed to operate the game controls, mouse, and keyboard. Focus and concentration are required to take in the action and react to everything going on. Clear communication is critical as players work with teammates to reach a goal or complete a quest.

When pro gamers stream their gameplay, comments and questions come in constantly. To handle both the game and the questions in the chat stream, pro gamers need to be able to quickly switch their attention from one task to another.

Comments in the chat might be negative, but gamers can't let it bother them. Calmness and mental toughness are required, even in stressful situations. Pro gamers need to stay in control of their emotions whether they're winning or losing.

17

Lee "Faker" Sang-hyeok, a top *League of Legends* player, describes life as a pro gamer as a "roller coaster" and says his unflappable nature helps him succeed. "I don't get mad easily," he says. "Everybody asks me, 'How do you manage your mental?' I said, 'I was just born like this.' At a recent personality test, they said I am a robot."[11]

Professional gamers can't be too stoic or aloof, however. Part of their appeal is the personality that comes through as they're playing, streaming, chatting. "Guys can relate to them," said professional basketball player Ben Simmons, an avid video game fan. "They are people you would hang with."[12]

Gamers need discipline to put in the hours of practice required to reach the top. In addition, because gaming is available 24/7, they must have the self-control to know when it's time to take a break for the good of their physical and mental health. "You can always stream more, when you aren't streaming you are losing out on potential revenue, potential growth, your viewers might be watching someone else (and maybe they won't come back),"[13] says Scott McMillan, founder of the Method esports organization. Time management techniques can be valuable in helping pro gamers create a schedule that supports both their health and career.

Working Conditions

Professional gamers don't head to an office when they go to work. They practice and stream from home or from a gaming house where they live with their teammates. Professional gamers spend much of their day in front of computer monitors. Seated in a comfortable gaming chair, they manipulate a gaming mouse, computer keyboard, or game controller to make onscreen moves. They wear a headset and microphone and may use a computer camera so they can appear onscreen while playing.

Members of a pro gaming team may live in a house with five or more team members. In addition to bedrooms and a kitchen, the house might have a gym where team members can work out.

It's Tough Being on Top

"Before winning the World Cup my identity was largely hidden since school was already out for the summer when I signed with 100 Thieves. Things were different when I started a new school in the fall. Suddenly because of my World Cup win, everyone knew who I was and the attention was overwhelming. I was stressed and miserable. I told my parents I wanted to transition to an online school. . . . My papá and my stepmom along with my three siblings understood how badly I wanted to go remote because they saw firsthand how unhappy I was. At first, my mamita resisted the idea. . . . Finally, after many discussions, it all worked out, and together we decided online school would be the best alternative for me and it has been.

I'm glad because my family is the most important thing in the world to me. Attending online school has given me a lot more flexibility in terms of my assignments and my schedule so I can continue to pursue gaming and still graduate high school this year."

—*Fortnite* player Arkhram (Diego Palma)

Quoted in Jenny Powers, "I'm a 17-year-old *Fortnite* Gamer Who's Won over $646,000 in Two Years Since Going Pro. I Average About 10 Hours of Gaming Daily," *Business Insider*, April 10, 2021. www.businessinsider.com.

The focal point of the house is the gaming room where computer stations are set up. This is where team members spend hours practicing and improving their skills.

Professional gamers earn money by streaming the content they create from their home or with their teammates. In addition, top professional gamers compete in tournaments held all over the world, from Los Angeles to Paris to Shanghai.

Employers and Earnings

Average annual pay for a video game player is $48,870 a year, according to ZipRecruiter. Top players can earn millions during their career, but the average yearly salary for professional players usually lands between $12,000 and $60,000 per year, according to Cyber Athletiks.com.

Sponsorships can be a significant source of revenue for professional gamers. Sponsors pay streamers and content creators to show ads on their streaming channels, wear clothes with a corporate brand, promote products on social media, and talk about and use products while they're playing. For example, Pokimane (real name: Imane Anys) made and ate Nissin noodles (a sponsor) while broadcasting her gameplay and chatting with fans.

Subscriptions are another way for professional gamers to earn money. Subscribers pay from four to ten dollars each month so they can see fewer ads, have priority in the chat, and unlock special chat emojis. The content creators get part of the subscription revenue.

To gain access to sponsors and gain more Twitch followers, a player may sign a contract with an esports team. The contract gives the team a percentage of the sponsorship money brought in by the player, and the player gains additional exposure and support by being connected with the team.

Future Outlook

Professional gaming is a new occupation that continues to grow. More leagues, such as NBA2K and Overwatch, are emerging. Twitch and other online platforms provide opportunities for streamers and gaming influencers to bring in revenue.

Although income from Twitch followers, YouTube content, and sponsorships is making it more common for people to be paid to play video games, it is still fairly rare for a person to play video games as a full-time job. McMillan, the Method founder, notes that players often begin by sharing their hobby with others online and working at it part-time before going to gaming full-time. "The gradual progression works well," he says, "and should give you an indication of whether this is something you can sustain and make a living from long term."[14]

Find Out More
Cloutboost
https://cloutboost.com/
This site uses data to help match sponsors with video game influencers.

FaZe Clan
www.fazeclan.com
An esports gaming organization that supports competitive gaming teams and content creators and offers fashion merchandise.

Method
Method.gg
This esports organization has a global platform for video game players and content creators.

National Esports Association
www.nea.gg
The organization provides development programs for esports athletes and offers gaming experiences.

QUALITY ASSURANCE TESTER

What Does a Quality Assurance Tester Do?

When Tony Sticks saw a job opening for a video game tester position, he thought it sounded fun. Game testers, also called quality assurance testers or quality assurance technicians, find flaws and bugs in video games so players aren't frustrated by them when they buy a game. They look for things that aren't working and report issues so problems can be corrected. Sticks was good at logic puzzles and breaking things, he told the person conducting the job interview. "They were quite surprised when I answered that [but] isn't that pretty much what a video game tester does?" he says. "You go in, you break things, you find bugs, and you report them."[15] Sticks got the job.

As they journey through a game, players may use objects, characters, and the environment in a multitude of ways. Quality assurance testers make sure the flow of the game is logical and consider whether or not a player's actions make sense. They look for surprising ways to play the game. This helps ensure that the game works even when a player does something the game designers didn't anticipate.

Testers don't just play games all day, however. They methodically work through sections of a game, looking for errors. When they find a bug they

---

A Few Facts

Typical Earnings
$40,483 annually*

Educational Requirements
High school diploma; associate's or bachelor's degree improves job opportunities

Personal qualities
Focus, perseverance, attention to detail

Work setting
Office, some opportunities to work remotely from home

* Average annual pay from PayScale, 2021

go through that section of the game multiple times to make sure it can be replicated. They then file a detailed report describing the issue. When a problem is fixed, testers check it again to make sure the game works as intended.

A Typical Workday

Quality assurance tester Jake King-Lee gets his testing tasks from the company's quality assurance lead. Testing time varies, anywhere from an hour to several days. A test plan lets King-Lee know what should happen in the game. He works through the game to make sure its features are performing as expected. "A simple example would be: There is a new button in the game. When the user clicks on the button it should go to a menu. If, during my test, when I click on the button the menu does not appear, or the game crashes, or something else happens, it should be reported as a bug,"[16] King-Lee explains.

Any errors he finds he reports to the person responsible for fixing them, usually the game's programmers. After they fix the problem, King-Lee tests that part of the game again to make sure things are working as they should. "Sometimes certain bugs can be really hard to fix so we will have to go back and forth lots of times before we fix it," says King-Lee. He adds, "This means that I will have to keep testing the same section of the game over and over and if it's not fixed I will have to report a bug. I have had experiences where certain bugs can take days to fix."[17]

Testers working on multiplayer games may also participate in stress tests. Stress tests are used to check for performance issues that could occur when a large number of users play the game at the same time. On these days, Sticks says, everyone in the office plays the multiplayer version of the game and tries to crash the servers. It is a chance to have fun with other people in the office, as well as test the system's limits.

Education and Training

There are generally no specific educational requirements needed to be a video game quality assurance tester. Having an associate's or bachelor's degree can be helpful in landing a job, however. A degree in computer programming, game design, software development, or a related field are good options. Jake King-Lee studied computer games development at a university and got a job as a quality assurance tester after graduating.

Quality assurance testers should be familiar with various databases, such as bug-tracking databases or test databases, as errors and issues are logged in a database. Because errors and bugs need to be explained and clearly communicated, technical writing courses can be helpful.

Courses in writing code and a bachelor's degree in computer science or computer engineering are also recommended and can help an individual move into a higher role as a software development engineer in test (which is the terminology used in the industry for this job). These programmers create automated tools for game testing and improve game testing processes. When a game has thousands of areas players can explore, it would be too cumbersome to test every possible action manually. A software development engineer in test writes code to move a character to thousands of areas in a game for a few seconds, in a fraction of the time it would take for someone to do this manually.

Skills and Personality

Quality assurance testers need to be familiar with how to play video games and can't be afraid to break them. Testers need to have an eye for detail and must be able to spot problems with how a game is played, how it looks, and how the characters move and act.

Perceptiveness, patience, and discipline are important qualities for video game testers. When a bug is discovered, they need to be able to isolate the issue and figure out what they did to cause the problem. This involves analyzing their actions and determining what caused the issue to occur. They also need to reproduce the bug, which involves patiently and methodically going

A Logical Choice

"If you are a logical person and like puzzles or finding solutions to hard problems, this might be the job for you. It is generally an easier job to get into in the gaming industry, but just because it is easier does not mean you cannot get a fulfilling career out of it. You can progress to higher QA [quality assurance] roles such as Lead QA. There is also QA Engineer roles where they write programs to help test. This would be good if you can also write code."

—Jake King-Lee, Quality Assurance Tester

Interview with author, May 15, 2021.

over the same part of the game again and again. "If when you play a game, you notice things that others don't, that is really useful," King-Lee said. "When you are testing you will generally be testing the same thing over and over. Everything might work perfectly but on the 100th time you test it something might go wrong. Being able to notice what you or the game did differently will help you in finding bugs that others might not."[18]

Communication skills are vital, as testers log and explain the problems they find. They might note that animation froze when a character punched an enemy, for example, or a player's health decreased instead of going up when a healing item was added. They must describe what they did to cause the glitch to occur. The description of the issue and how it happened must be clear and easy to understand because programmers use information logged by the testers to fix problems.

To create the best game experience for players, video game testers need to approach their work with a good attitude. Testing may involve replaying the same section of a game multiple times, and video game testers need to maintain a positive approach

Aching to Move

"You're basically sitting at a desk all day, and if you're playing video games 12 hours a day six days a week, you're in a stationary position with your controller. Sometimes you have nice seats and you can kick back a little bit. But you can really only do that so much before your body starts aching. I would get home from being a video game tester and the only thing I wanted to do was move. I wanted to run, I wanted to lift weights, I wanted to work out because I couldn't stand not moving."

—Tony Sticks, former video game tester

Tony Sticks, "What It's Really Like to Be a Video Game Tester," YouTube, August 8, 2020. www.youtube.com/watch?v=fz_1i-qLg0k.

toward their work even when it becomes tedious. Because they work as part of the game development team, testers also need to collaborate and maintain a good rapport with coworkers.

Working Conditions

Quality assurance testers usually work in an office setting, although some may work remotely and log into the company's systems from home. The dress code is usually casual, and free coffee and soda are commonly provided in the office. The office environment can be fun and upbeat, as everyone there has a shared interest in video games. "There are artists, animators, designers, programmers, and testers, but what they all have in common is that they love games and love making games," King-Lee says, adding, "We often have fun work activities or celebrations at work when we reach milestones. It's a good place to work."[19]

When the deadline for a new game release nears, the work environment can become stressful, and quality assurance testers may find themselves working overtime. They may be expected to work twelve-hour days six days a week to make sure the game is ready for release on time. These crunch periods can take a toll on a tester's health and social life.

Employers and Earnings

The position of video game quality assurance tester is often a first job for a person looking for a career in the video game industry. A quality assurance tester might be hired by a game studio or by a temporary agency that has a contract with the game studio. Job openings for this position can be found on game studio websites as well as online job search websites.

Pay for video game quality assurance testers in 2021 ranged from around $18,000 to about $55,000 per year, according to the Game Industry Career Guide. PayScale put the average annual salary at $40,483.

Pay is generally based on company size and location, and whether a tester is a contractor or an employee. A quality assurance tester can advance to other roles, such as lead tester, which had a 2021 pay range of $50,000 to $58,000 per year, according to Game Industry Career Guide.

A job as a video game tester can be insecure, as a tester's job may be eliminated after a game has been launched. However, growth in the video game industry due to an interest in multiplayer games and mobile games means new job opportunities are plentiful.

Find Out More

Game Industry Career Guide
www.gameindustrycareerguide.com
This website offers numerous articles about game industry careers and education. It includes an overview of a video game quality assurance tester's job duties and offers insights on how to get hired. In addition, job opening information and general job hunting tips are provided, including articles on résumés, applying for jobs, interviewing, and networking.

GamesIndustry.biz Academy

www.gamesindustry.biz/academy

This website features articles for people working in the video game industry. It provides information about making, selling, and working in games. Articles dive into topics such as fixing bugs, game development, and developing a game's narrative.

Kotaku

https://kotaku.com/

This website offers news, game reviews, and interviews with people in the gaming industry.

DRONE PILOT

What Does a Drone Pilot Do?

It's still dark when Chris Hibben and his crew set up for an early-morning drone flight. They're getting ready to capture the sun's rays as they emerge over the horizon. "A lot of times people want that early morning sunrise shot, so we get up at the crack of dawn, 3 a.m., before the sun is out," Hibben says. "We get everything set up in the dark and then wait for the sun to come up. Everybody loves the golden hours."[20] Hibben, owner of Snap 180 Media, is a drone pilot and owner of a video production company that specializes in getting a bird's-eye view of whatever his clients want. The footage is used for commercials as well as news and sports broadcasts.

Drone pilots fly unmanned aerial vehicles, or UAVs, more commonly known as drones. They use a remote control to maneuver the drone as it flies. A screen, smartphone, or tablet plugged into the controller gives the operator a view of the landscape the drone is flying over.

In addition to recording video for broadcasts and commercials, a drone can snap pictures that are used to create maps showing a site's features and elevation. Drones may deliver packages or medicine, provide video for a roof inspection, or locate areas of a farm field that need water. They might

---

A Few Facts

Typical Earnings
$58,280 annually*

Educational Requirements
Remote pilot certificate

Personal Qualities
Patient, adaptable, inquisitive, dedicated, focused, persevering

Work Settings
Outdoors when flying, in an office when planning flights and working with data

* Average annual pay from ZipRecruiter, 2021

---

be equipped with a heat-sensing system used to find a lost hiker. The military uses drones for overseas military missions as well as search-and-rescue operations.

Civil engineer and drone pilot Tony Carmody uses a drone to do site surveys, take pictures, and collect data. This information is used to create a mosaic photo or 3-D model of an area that's targeted for a construction project. "It's a top-down view of the site as it was surveyed that day," he says. "The 3D model puts them in the middle of the site and lets them walk the project site without even leaving their desk."[21]

A Typical Workday

Carmody's flights begin in the office. He plans the mission there, doing research to see whether government clearance is needed to fly in the area being surveyed. He considers what he wants to get out of the mission and designs a flight plan. He transfers the plan to the drone so that it has instructions for taking photos at certain altitudes.

Once Carmody gets to the site, he sets out targets to use as control points. Because he knows the elevation of these points, they provide a frame of reference in the drone's images. He makes adjustments to the flight plan based on what he sees on the site. Then he sends the drone up. "Most drone flights are less than an hour," he says. "We can be on site and off site in less than half a day."[22] The time savings is considerable when compared to the day or two it would have taken to do a manual survey of the same site.

Hibben also begins his flights with a day of preparation. He checks the weather to make sure it will work for the flight and tunes up his equipment. "You make sure software and firmware are updated, and the batteries are charged,"[23] he says.

Hibben and his crew might operate the drone for a full day, making sure the flight path and images are just right. Crew members watch for birds that might attack the drone, and they make sure the drone isn't heading for trees. They also manipulate spe-

Watch Out for Birds!

"The worst part is seagulls. Seagulls hate drones and they dive at them all the time. If they come at you, you need to stop in mid-air and then bank out of the way. You hide and wait for them to leave."

—Drone pilot Chris Hibben, owner of Snap 180 Media

Interview with the author, June 18, 2021.

cial equipment called a gimbal that's attached to the drone and allows the camera to swivel. "We fly in multiple flight paths, and use the gimbal to give it that cool, cinematic look,"[24] Hibben says.

Education and Training

Commercial drone pilots need a Remote Pilot Certificate from the Federal Aviation Administration (FAA). The certificate shows that a person understands the regulations that dictate safety and other aspects of operating drones.

To become eligible for certification, individuals need to be at least sixteen years old and be able to read, write, speak, and understand English. They must be physically and mentally capable of safely flying a drone. Before registering for the test, they create an Integrated Airman Certification and Rating Application (IACRA) profile online. The application is used to make sure applicants meet regulatory requirements.

To become certified, individuals must pass the Remote Pilot Knowledge Test, which is given at a regional testing center. The test covers flight safety and regulations, including flight restrictions, operating requirements, how weather impacts flight, emergency procedures, and radio communication. It also goes over maintenance, preflight inspections, and decision-making.

A drone pilot uses his equipment to inspect work being done at a construction site. Drones can be used for site surveys, data collection, and to record activity through photos and videos.

Once they're certified, drone pilots need to stay up-to-date on aviation knowledge. Every twenty-four months, certificate holders must complete an online training course.

Individuals can study for the knowledge test on their own or take a class to help them prepare. Classes are available through organizations such as Drone Pilot Ground School or the University of Delaware's Professional Drone Pilot Training Academy. For those studying on their own, the FAA provides online study materials.

In-depth training and comprehensive drone education are available through the Unmanned Aircraft System Operations program at the University of North Dakota. This bachelor's degree program provides experience with drones of all sizes and information about the safety and operations requirements of the National Airspace System.

Practice flying the drone itself is the best way to become skilled at operating it. Flying a drone as a hobby led Rachel Gilmore, owner of the drone company FloridaProFly, to a career as a professional drone pilot. She learned mapping and flying skills while living in the Virgin Islands, where flying drones in the mountainous terrain taught her how to navigate in challenging conditions. "I practiced every week, often on the golf course and out over the ocean," she says. "I practiced until I understood exactly how to do the maps, exactly how to make the models, and how to make them perfect."[25]

Skills and Personality

Drone pilots need the mechanical skills necessary to maintain the drone and excellent hand-eye coordination to operate it. Dexterity is needed to manipulate the controller, and pilots need to understand how their movements impact what the drone is doing.

Drone pilots need to be patient, detail oriented, and organized. They need to create a flight plan that takes the flight goal, regulations, and safety considerations into account. They need to be patient and be ready to solve problems when they get onsite. If temperatures are low, for example, they need to consider whether ice might form on the drone and cause it to crash and thus adjust their plan for the day accordingly.

Skills in photography, film editing, color correction, and graphics can be beneficial for drone operators. Hibben has been doing photography and videography since the age of eleven, flies remote-control airplanes as a hobby, and has his pilot's license. "That interest in aviation and remote control devices and video games allowed me to excel on the drone side,"[26] he says.

Working Conditions

Drone pilots plan their flights in an indoor office and then operate the drone outdoors. They travel to the event, field, or construc-

Have a Plan, and Be Ready to Change It

"With technology it's never perfect, there's a lot of troubleshooting to think through. Even though you plan from the office and think you're good to go, when you get on site the terrain may be different. Be patient and use your thought process, 'I have a problem and how am I going to fix it?' If something doesn't go your way, try and fix it and come up with a new game plan rather than waving the white flag [of surrender]."

—Tony Carmody, drone pilot and civil engineer

Interview with the author, July 9, 2021.

tion site that needs to be mapped or filmed. Carmody enjoys the opportunity to balance time spent in the office with time on the work site.

For Hibben, getting to the work site means spending hours in his truck as he travels to a business's location or sporting or news event. "I'm on the road a lot and spend a lot of time in my Suburban, driving from place to place,"[27] he says

Hibben stores his drones in a shop where he has everything needed to keep the equipment in top shape: a workbench, soldering tools, wrenches, and screwdrivers. He also has a generator that's taken to sites, such as golf courses, where there are no electrical outlets for charging batteries.

Employers and Earnings

Drone pilots earn an average of $58,280 per year, with the majority of drone pilots earning between $40,000 and $68,000 annually. Salaries range from $22,000 to $126,500 a year, according to ZipRecruiter.

Drone pilots might be self-employed, have their own company, or do drone work as part of another job. Gilmore's drone company makes maps for clients, while drones are an additional tool for Hibben's photography and videography company. Carmody, a civil engineer, says being a drone pilot is an asset to his career and the company he works for. "Once I got that drone license we were able to add that to another line of work that we do,"[28] he says.

The FAA expects the need for drone pilots to greatly increase. It expects 350,000 individuals to be certified as remote pilots by 2025, up from 206,000 in 2020. The need may be even greater as drones become more efficient and battery life is extended.

Find Out More

Aircraft Owners and Pilots Association
www.aopa.org/go-fly/drones
This website for pilots provides news on drones, training information, and job contacts.

Federal Aviation Administration
Certified Remote Pilots Including Commercial Operators
www.faa.gov/uas/commercial_operators/
This website outlines the steps to becoming a certified drone pilot. It includes links to study materials for the knowledge test.

University of North Dakota
Unmanned Aircraft System Operations
https://und.edu/programs/unmanned-aircraft-system-operations
-bs-aero/index.html
This bachelor's degree program from the University of North Dakota prepares students to work as a pilot, sensor operator, or member of an unmanned aircraft systems team. It is part of the Federal Aviation Administration's Unmanned Aircraft Systems Collegiate Training Initiative program.

GAME ARTIST

What Does a Game Artist Do?

Game artists and animators make the visual elements of a video game. They create a game's visual style, whether it's designed to look like the real world or an imaginary one, and create characters, vehicles, objects, and landscapes. They bring characters to life by giving them features, moves, and emotions.

When 3-D animator Arthur Munoz designs a character, he first decides how to describe it. "I always start by giving some keywords to define the character and what kind of 'energy' I'm looking for," says Munoz, who has worked on *Steelrising*, *Technomancer*, and *Greedfall* from Spider Games. "These keywords will be the anchors for this character."[29] He then looks for images that have those elements and uses them for reference as he brings the character to life.

Artists like Munoz who work in 3-D get direction on the game's look and style from concept artists. Concept artists work with a game's producer or art director to understand the vision for the game. They create ideas that shape the look of the game's environment. "I'll usually do three different ideas that show the potential direction to take," says concept artist Roger Adams, who works for Digital Extremes on the *Warframe* game. "You don't need a lot, you just need something good."[30]

A Few Facts

Typical Earnings
Average annual salary:
$69,194*

Educational Requirements
Bachelor's degree in computer graphics, art, or a related field

Personal Qualities
Artistic talent, creativity, communication skills, organizational skills

Work Settings
Office

* Average annual pay from ZipRecruiter, 2021

After 3-D modelers use software to create the character, vehicle, or other items in the game's environment, details are added by a 2-D texture artist. Artists also work with lighting to adjust the colors and intensity to create the game's mood and add details such as weather effects. In addition, artists create the game's background and setting, adding pillars, floors, walls, and signs.

Animators make characters move in the game. Short animations show characters running, talking, walking, or climbing. These brief animations play one after another and look like one continuous scene, as the game engine rapidly pulls them into the game. Artists also create longer animated scenes, which are like short animated movies.

A Typical Workday

Game artists spend much of their day creating computer-generated (CG) art but also spend time in meetings, doing research, and talking with team members. They communicate with game designers, programmers, audio engineers, and other artists to stay on top of the game's progress. They must meet deadlines, fix problems, and understand what will be needed as game creation moves forward.

Matt Collins, a CG supervisor for Forza Motorsport at Microsoft, estimates that about 60 percent of a game artist's day is spent using computer programs to create 3-D art. A game artist's day begins with a brief meeting. "In the morning we have a huddle to talk about the problems of the day, what did we do yesterday, what's the plan for today, and is there anything we need to chase down,"[31] Collins says.

From there, artists might go to meetings that focus on a specific game feature or work on creating art. As a supervisor, Collins prioritizes and identifies graphic features used in the game and works with his team to make sure the features are implemented across the game. Collins also works with the production team to make sure the graphics work smoothly with the game itself.

Game artists have busy days, and it's important for them to speak up, ask questions, and communicate with other members to understand what should be handled first. "There will be a lot of different things coming at you and you need to sort through the noise," Collins says. "There is a lot of prioritizing of your time."[32]

Education and Training

Game artists typically have a bachelor's degree in computer graphics, art, or a related field. They also create a portfolio of their work that shows their abilities and style.

Barbara Bernad, a 3-D animator who has worked on the *Hitman* video game series, for example, studied drawing, typography, illustration, and photography in high school. In college she found art history to be a valuable course, as she gained insights by seeing and analyzing the styles and techniques of other artists. While she also learned 3-D animation in college, she found a good foundation in fine art (where she learned drawing, composition, and sculpting) to be important.

Collins attended DigiPen Institute of Technology for two years after graduating from a four-year art program in New Hampshire. Many game artists get a two- or four-year degree where they study game creation as well as traditional art courses, Collins says, but online training is becoming more common.

It's important for video game animators to learn how game engines operate and understand how the images they are creating will work within the game. Before adding features and details, animators use rigging techniques to create a character's skeleton or structure for a 3-D model. The object's or character's movements can then be controlled. As technology is continually changing, artists keep learning while on the job. When making creatures for the game *Greedfall*, Munoz worked to find ways to make them move more fluidly. "I learned the basics of animation as a student, but most of my knowledge came from working as

Making It Real

"I usually do some research, see how certain things and their movements look in reality, or I may simply stand in front of the mirror and act it out. There are times in which I may video record myself in order to see the mechanics of movements.

Go out and look at people on the street, the way they walk and talk, the way they move their hands. Go to places where people go jogging. Look at how the proportion of their body affects their movements. Pay attention; make sketches, watch videos, practice, practice, and practice some more."

—Barbara Bernad, 3-D animator

Quoted in Tammi Edwards, "Interview with Barbara Bernad—3D Animator & Video Game Developer," The Art Career Project, November 28, 2018. www.theartcareerproject.com.

a professional animator," he says, adding, "Each game and character to animate is a good occasion to enhance your skills and understand animation."[33]

Skills and Personality

Game artists need to have artistic talent and the technical skills necessary to express that talent. They need to know the fundamentals of shape, color, and composition and how to use computer programs. They need to be creative, as they may need to invent new worlds or creatures, and they need to be focused, persistent, and detailed to make their ideas work within the game. Being observant is a good quality as well. Understanding how people, vehicles, and animals move is essential to re-creating that movement in a game.

Because graphics must blend in seamlessly with the game, game artists need to have a solid grasp of the game's animation

Game artists spend much of their day working with team members. They communicate with game designers, programmers, audio engineers, and other artists to stay on top of the game's progress.

system. The way a character or vehicle moves or pauses must feel right to the person playing the game. A heavy vehicle needs to lumber along more slowly, while a sleek sports car has to spin and turn with precision. A glitch in the animation can ruin the player's experience, so game artists and animators need to do whatever they can to make sure that doesn't happen. "Gameplay is always the 'king' of the game, no matter how cool your animations are," Munoz says. "So, keep it simple, clear, and always play the game [yourself] to see how it feels."[34]

Communication skills are critical for game artists and animators. They need to listen and understand a project's requirements, ask questions, and talk with team members to solve problems and make sure everyone is moving in the same direction. Having a positive attitude is important, especially when deadlines near and stress levels rise.

Working Conditions

Game artists and animators work in an office as part of a team. A sense of camaraderie often develops as artists collaborate on a project. Collins notes that his team of artists is always trying to improve the game while meeting deadlines, which brings pressure but also leads to some creative problem solving. "There's an adrenaline that comes with that," Collins says. "Your mind is always working. It's really engaging; you never get bored."[35]

As part of a game development team, artists and animators need to work according to the project timeline. If setbacks occur, this can mean working overtime (referred to as *crunch* in the industry) as deadlines approach. However, planning and building in time for unexpected events can help a team avoid the long hours associated with crunch.

Employers and Earnings

Game artists, who create 2-D and 3-D elements for a game, make an average of $69,194 a year, according to ZipRecruiter's 2021 data. Salaries range from $16,500 to $143,000 annually. Game animators, who make characters move in a video game, make an average of $51,259 a year. Salaries for animators range from $27,000 at the low end to a high of $103,500.

Game artists and animators often work for game development companies. Those who work for smaller companies often have a wider variety of work, while those at a larger company will usually be more specialized. Artists who work as freelancers are usually hired to create artwork for a specific project.

Future Outlook

The job outlook for special effects artists and animators (the category in which game artists fall) is expected to grow by 4 percent by 2029, about as fast as average, according to the Bureau of Labor Statistics. There will be an increase in demand for people

Get to Know Your Monster

"Even monsters can have a backstory and a personality, so it's important to give them one before animating. Give them secondary actions, to show their personality and their behavior, like a scream before charging or pointing at his opponent with his sword before an attack. It's also a good feedback for the player to anticipate and learn the pattern of his opponent."

—Arthur Munoz, 3-D animator

Quoted in Krill Tokarev, "Insight into Character Animation for Games from Arthur Munoz," 80 Level, no date. https://80.lv.

who can create visual effects for video games, although some companies may hire people outside the United States who can work for less pay.

There are computer programs that are able to create automated graphics. Rather than hurting the job outlook, this provides new opportunities for artists who learn how to work with the new programs. "Art is always needed," Collins explains. "You're not going to replace art with computers."[36]

Find Out More
The Art Career Project
https://www.theartcareerproject.com/
This website provides emerging artists with information about careers, schools, and scholarships. It offers college rankings and a variety of art career guides, including information on digital arts.

Destiny Gaming
https://destinygamingblogs.com/
Interviews with people who work in the video game industry are featured on this website. It also includes video game reviews and historic information on video game consoles.

80 Level

https://80.lv/

80 Level provides a platform for digital artists, animators, game developers, and people who just love video games. Its articles offer technical information on designing video game artwork. The site also has links to courses and workshops in 3-D modeling and other skills.

International Game Developers Association

https://igda.org/

This organization is for individuals who work with game creation. It offers career resources and online communities for individuals interested in various aspects of game creation, including art.

AUDIO ENGINEER

What Does an Audio Engineer Do?

Video games are filled with thousands of sounds. Sound gives a game style, tone, and drama, letting players know when they're in danger and when they're on a roll. Music sets the mood, motors rev and roar, and an explosion of strength and energy reverberates when a character powers up. Thanks to the work of an audio engineer, these sounds perfectly capture the moment and immerse a player in the game.

Audio engineers use creativity, ingenuity, and technical know-how to create distinct and dramatic sounds. A light saber sounds different than a blaster in a *Star Wars* game, and harvesting carrots sounds different than mining diamonds in *Minecraft*. You can tell by the music and sound effects whether someone is playing *Grand Theft Auto*, *Forza Motorsport*, or *Mario Cart*. The sounds of triumph are different from those of defeat. This brings variety to an audio engineer's work. "My favorite part of my job is how varied my work is from day to day," explains Chase Thompson, who has worked on *Halo*, *Fable*, and *Star Wars*. "One day I might be implementing game music for a new multiplayer mode, the next I might be fixing a bug with one of the vehicle

A Few Facts

Typical Earnings
$53,520 per year*

Educational Requirements
Training and practical experience in using audio technology, associate's or bachelor's degree

Personal Qualities
Problem-solving skills, creative, communication skills, calm in stressful situations

Work Settings
Office or sound studio; on-site for live sound recordings.

* Median pay for sound engineering technicians, Bureau of Labor Statistics, 2020

sounds, and the next I might be helping design new and exciting technology with our programming teams."[37]

Because a game's sounds are vital to immersing a player in the game, they need to have a realistic feel. That was Seph Lawrence's goal when he worked on sound effects for the *Diablo* games. "Even though it's a world built on fantasy . . . I wanted the sound of the game to have a certain quality of realism if at all possible," Lawrence explains. "As if someone walked up to you in a supermarket parking lot and launched an arcane projectile, you might find the sound believable."[38]

A Typical Workday

Audio engineers use recording equipment to record sounds in a studio and on-site. They use technology to mix and layer the sounds as they work to find the sound that perfectly suits a game's situation. Computer programs are used to sync sounds with action and make sure they capture the spirit of the game and the character's movements.

When recording, engineers may work in the studio to record dialogue and voices or go out on location to capture other sounds. Before heading out on location, they must understand what they need to get out of the recording session, whether that's the sound of rushing water or the boom of an explosion. Planning is essential to making the most of their time on-site.

When recording on location, audio engineers set up microphones and record from a variety of vantage points to get different perspectives on the sound. They may need to troubleshoot on-site, as equipment can malfunction, and they do a variety of takes to make sure they have what they need when they get back to the studio. Noise from birds, insects, traffic, or the wind can all interfere with the sound they're trying to record. "Often, you will not know until you are in the studio which mics/perspectives work best for the sounds you are trying to design," notes audio engineer Chuck Russom, who has worked on *Medal of Honor* and *Call of Duty*. "So it is to your benefit to record with as many different mics set up in as many different positions as possible."[39]

Lawrence's work on *Diablo* required recording everything from water and animals to spectacular noises. "We dropped a huge boulder on a car," he says, "and rode a coasting bulldozer down a hill to record the sound of the clanking treads."[40]

In the studio, various sounds are layered using audio software. Audio engineers use software to create the distinct sounds that are needed. After the sounds are ready, they're merged with the game and tested in gameplay.

Education and Training

Audio engineers must be familiar with computer programs and the equipment used to create audio files. An associate's or bachelor's degree may be required for some jobs.

Because technology is constantly evolving, audio technicians often take continuing education courses or receive on-the-job training in the latest programs and hardware. "I think most people who don't already know about game development are surprised at how technical the job is,"[41] says video game sound designer Jaclyn Shumate, who has worked on *Peggle 2* and *Star Wars Kinect*.

Courses in coding can give audio engineers an understanding of how games are built. This knowledge is important when working with programmers and other team members who are working to build a game. "If none of you have any idea of what the other person is talking about, this can get problematic once the deadline is approaching and the stress kicks in," notes musical composer and video game audio freelancer Ted Wennerstrom.[42]

It takes hours of practice to learn to be an audio engineer, and one way to work on the necessary skills is to record sounds and manipulate them with a free audio software program. Tutorials provide lessons on how to use the program, and from there users can experiment with the sounds and build a prototype project.

Always Ready

"I make a point of always having my recording rigs ready to grab and go at a moment's notice so I don't miss anything that occurs spontaneously. In this same spirit, I usually keep a handheld recorder in the glove box of my car.

Whenever I'm sick with a stuffy nose and sore throat, I always try to get in front of a mic and record some snorting, scratchy, throaty goo noise that only happens when you are sick. This stuff can be solid gold for making monster SFX. It can certainly feel like the last thing in the world you'd want to do when you aren't feeling well but you'll thank yourself later for the sacrifice."

—Sound designer Seph Lawrence

Quoted in Philip Mantione, "Interview with Veteran Sound Designer: Seph Lawrence," Pro Audio Files, September 4, 2018. https://theproaudiofiles.com.

Skills and Personality

An audio engineer needs to be organized, creative, persistent, and a good collaborator. A game's sounds support other elements of the game, from characters to mood to action, and audio engineers need to communicate with team members to understand which sounds are needed and how they fit in. They need to be good listeners and ask questions to figure out what will work best in a given situation.

Audio engineers must be patient, as capturing the sound they're looking for is likely to take numerous attempts. They also need to be organized and aware of deadlines. Because there are endless ways to create sounds, audio engineers must sort through options, choose the best one, and know when it's time to move on. Games are created on a schedule, and audio engineers must make sure the game's audio features are ready on time.

Audio engineers create and mix the sounds that give video games their style and tone as well as helping to make the action feel realistic. These sounds can also add drama, humor, or suspense to the games.

In addition to understanding how to use recording equipment, audio engineers should also know how to repair the equipment. When problems arise, they need to think critically and use logic and calmly work to find a solution. "Very often things can get intense and stressful near deadlines," Lawrence says. "The stakes are often high and in those moments I want to be surrounded by level-headed professionals who are able to keep their cool when things get tough and perform at a high level while still maintaining their composure and sense of humor."[43]

Creativity is also an asset for an audio engineer. Games can require unique sounds, and audio engineers might find inspiration when taking a walk or a drive. Lawrence sometimes captures unique sounds by placing a microphone close to a soft sound, such as a credit card being scraped across a carpet or a piece of cloth.

Working Conditions

Audio engineers typically mix sounds and sync them with a game while working in an office or recording studio. When audio engineers are recording, they may travel to an outside location. They might go to a shooting range to record gunshots or a nature center to capture the sound of a rushing river or rustling leaves.

An audio engineer's schedule mirrors that of others working on the game. When deadlines near, they need to work long hours to get the final product to sound just right.

Employers and Earnings

The median pay for audio engineers is $53,520, according to the US Bureau of Labor Statistics. They might work for a large company that creates games, or they may work independently as a freelancer. Working for a video game company provides exposure to the game development process, as well as a steady paycheck. The engineer has access to the studio's equipment and software.

Freelancers have more control over their schedule and the projects they work on; however, they need their own equipment and workspace. They need to be self-motivated and find another project when one is completed. It is also helpful for freelancers to have a unique talent that sets them apart from others, as this provides an advantage when competing for jobs. Wennerstrom found that having the ability to shift sound effects in relation to the game's action helped him find work. "This gave me a clear advantage and a good selling point when I looked for work," he explains. "And the companies love it when I show it to them."[44]

The Best Part

"My favorite part of my job is watching something that I've worked on so hard finally come to life, and knowing that it may make other people feel as good as it made me feel over the development process. Getting to do a final mix for a game, and realizing it sounds like what you've been imagining in your head for months (or years, in some cases) is one of my happiest work- and artistic moments."

—Video game sound designer Jaclyn Shumate

Quoted in Jason W. Bay, "How to Become a Video Game Sound Designer," Video Game Career Guide, no date. www.gameindustrycareerguide.com.

Future Outlook

Jobs for sound engineering technicians are expected to grow faster than average, according to the Bureau of Labor Statistics. By 2029, jobs are expected to increase by 6 percent.

Practicing with audio programs and creating new material can prepare a person for a career as an audio engineer. A production company or studio that needs part-time help can be a good place to get experience. "Do everything you can to learn about sound design and audio implementation," Shumate advises. "It takes a lot of practice! Seek feedback, be open to it, and put together a killer demo."[45]

Find Out More

Audio Engineering Society

www.aes.org/

This international organization for audio engineers provides industry news and information about audio research and technology. It offers tutorials and networking opportunities.

Game Industry Career Guide

www.gameindustrycareerguide.com

This website provides insights into a variety of careers in the video game industry. It features interviews with individuals working in the industry and offers links to training resources.

ScreenSkills

www.screenskills.com

This London-based website provides information about careers in the video game industry, including careers in sound design. It offers job profiles in the game industry, as well as film and visual effects. It also provides links to training opportunities.

SOURCE NOTES

Introduction: Connecting with a Growing Industry

1. Quoted in Carro Mackenzie, "How *Animal Crossing* Conquered the World: A Delightful Video Game Helped Millions of Americans Through a Challenging Time," *Scholastic Scope*, September 2020, p. 25.
2. Quoted in Jason Bay, "Why Should You Work at a Mobile Game Company?," Game Industry Career Guide, 2021. www.gameindustrycareerguide.com.
3. Mojan Ahmadi, author interview, May 13, 2021.
4. Quoted in Entertainment Software Association, "Meet Sloane Miller, an ESA Foundation Computer and Video Game Arts and Sciences Scholar," February 24, 2021. www. theesa.com.

Game Designer

5. Quoted in Jason W. Bay, "How to Become a Video Game Designer," Game Industry Career Guide, 2021. www.game industrycareerguide.com.
6. Quoted in Jaclyn Walsh, "10 Skills You Need to Become a Video Game Designer," Peterson's, March 27, 2020. www .petersons.com.
7. Quoted in Walsh, "10 Skills You Need to Become a Video Game Designer."

Professional Gamer

8. Quoted in Jenny Powers, "I'm a 17-year-old *Fortnite* Gamer Who's Won over $646,000 in Two Years Since Going Pro. I Average About 10 Hours of Gaming Daily," *Business Insider*, April 10, 2021. www.businessinsider.com.
9. Quoted in Intel, "The Daily Regimen of Players in Professional Gaming, " Intel.com, no date. www.intel.com.
10. Quoted in Bence Loksa, "How To Be a Nurse and a Female Pro Gamer at the Same Time—An Interview with Emmalee

'EMUHLEET' Garrido," ESTNN, June 12, 2021. https://estnn.com.

11. Quoted in Xing Li, "Faker: 'Living as a Progamer Is like a Roller Coaster,'" Dot Esports, July 8, 2019. https://dotesports.com.

12. Quoted in Rohan Nadkarni, "The Stream Team," *Sports Illustrated*, July 2021, p. 32.

13. Quoted in Polina Haryacha, "Interview with WoW Twitch Streamer & Pro Gamer Scott McMillan," Cloutboost, no date. https://cloutboost.com.

14. Haryacha, "Interview with WoW Twitch Streamer & Pro Gamer Scott McMillan."

Quality Assurance Tester

15. Tony Sticks, "What It's Really Like to Be a Video Game Tester," YouTube, August 8, 2020. www.youtube.com.

16. Jake King-Lee, interview with the author, May 15, 2021.

17. King-Lee, interview with the author.

18. King-Lee, interview with the author.

19. King-Lee, interview with the author.

Drone Pilot

20. Chris Hibben, interview with the author, June 18, 2021.

21. Tony Carmody, interview with the author, July 9, 2021.

22. Carmody, interview with the author.

23. Hibben, interview with the author.

24. Hibben, interview with the author.

25. Quoted in Zacc Dukowitz, "Building a Drone Services Business That Will Last: An Interview with Rachel Gilmore, Founder of Florida ProFly Drone Services," UAV Coach, July 12, 2018. https://uavcoach.com.

26. Hibben, interview with the author.

27. HIbben, interview with the author.

28. Carmody, interview with the author.

Game Artist

29. Quoted in Krill Tokarev, "Insight into Character Animation for Games from Arthur Munoz," 80 Level, no date. https://80.lv.

30. Quoted in Zay Altick, "Focus on What You Love and Do It the Very Best You Can at This Moment in Time—Roger Adams," Destiny Gaming, July 2020. https://destinygamingblogs.com.
31. Matt Collins, interview with the author, July 20, 2021.
32. Collins, interview with the author.
33. Quoted in Tokarev, "Insight into Character Animation for Games from Arthur Munoz."
34. Quoted in Tokarev, "Insight into Character Animation for Games from Arthur Munoz."
35. Collins, interview with the author.
36. Collins, interview with the author.

Audio Engineer

37. Quoted in Jason W. Bay, "How to Become a Video Game Audio Implementor," Game Industry Career Guide, no date. www.gameindustrycareerguide.com.
38. Quoted in Philip Mantione, "Interview with Veteran Sound Designer: Seph Lawrence," Pro Audio Files, September 4, 2018. https://theproaudiofiles.com.
39. Quoted in George Spanos, "Game Sound Design Interviews Chuck Russom," Game Sound Design, no date. http://gamesounddesign.com.
40. Quoted in Mantione, "Interview with Veteran Sound Designer: Seph Lawrence."
41. Quoted in Jason W. Bay, "How to Become a Video Game Sound Designer," Video Game Career Guide, no date. www.gameindustrycareerguide.com.
42. Quoted in Jason W. Bay, "My Life as a Video Game Audio Freelancer: What I Wish I Knew Starting Out," Game Industry Career Guide, no date. www.gameindustrycareerguide.com/video-game-audio-freelancer-what-i-wish-i-knew/.
43. Quoted in Mantione, "Interview with Veteran Sound Designer: Seph Lawrence."
44. Quoted in Bay, "My Life as a Video Game Audio Freelancer."
45. Quoted in Bay, "How to Become a Video Game Sound Designer."

INTERVIEW WITH A PROFESSIONAL GAMER

James "Firebat" Kostesich is a professional video game player. He competes in tournaments and streams his gameplay on Twitch and YouTube. He won the Hearthstone World Championship in 2014, and answered questions about his career by email.

Q: What is your job title?
A: My job goes by a lot of titles. For a while I was called an influencer, then content creator, and now finally streamer/YouTuber. Which basically means I make content on Twitch.tv and YouTube.

Q: Why did you choose this career?
A: I didn't really.

Q: Then how did you get into this field?
A: I liked playing games online so much that I just did it all the time and eventually started to get good at it. Then I won a few small tournaments, then a world championship. Everyone around me kind of pressured me into doing it, and I really didn't want to. I hate talking in front of people, let alone having a camera on me all day while strangers get to comment on me. But after I won *Worlds* [*2014 BlizzCon World Championship*] I was getting lots of offers to join esports teams, and they all had contracts that I stream my practice games. So, then I ended up signing one, moving to Texas, and living in a team house with other streamers/gamers. I was pulling in like 10k+ concurrent viewers back then and only getting paid $3,000 a month because I had no idea what I was doing. That kind of viewership is easily worth 3 to 4 times that. But that's kind of how most people get started.

Q: What is your typical workday like?
A: I usually try to stream in the morning so I have a lot of energy, and I try to stream as long as possible, but after 4 to 5 hours it's pretty tough to keep being engaged playing the same game and answering the same questions over and over. Then I edit down a good 10-minute clip from the stream to turn into the YouTube video for the day. I sometimes go to meet with ad people about doing some ads on the channel or stream.

Q: What do you like most about your job?
A: I get to set my own schedule and I can work from home. And sometimes I get to travel to cool events. And sometimes I get to make connections with viewers.

Q: What do you like least about your job?
A: Dealing with harassment. Dealing with being a public figure and having everyone judging my every opinion on everything. All the political stuff. Being attacked by viewers who blame me any time [the company that makes the game I play] makes a decision that makes them unhappy. People have a hard time understanding that just because I make content for a game doesn't mean I actually work for the company. Recently [the company] made a lot of decisions that made the game more expensive and so people went ballistic for months.

Q: What is the workplace atmosphere like?
A: Well, it's my spare bedroom.

Q: What personal qualities do you find most valuable for this type of work?
A: Persistence and the ability to tolerate people.

Q: What advice do you have for students who might be interested in this career?
A: I suggest creating content as a hobby and keeping a solid career path lined up. Success is determined a lot more by luck than anything else.

OTHER JOBS IF YOU LIKE VIDEO GAMES

App developer
Audio technician
Brand director
Broadcast engineer
Business development
Community manager
Computer programmer
Content designer
Content writer
Copywriter
Customer support
Data analyst
Data architect
Database administrator
Digital architect
Digital designer
Film editor
Game marketer
Game writer
Information technology analyst
Information technology consultant

Information technology sales professional
Marketing manager
Multimedia programmer
Network architect
Network engineer
Programming engineer
Script writer
Search engine optimization specialist
Social media manager
Software developer
Software engineer
Sound technician
Systems analyst
Systems designer
Technical support specialist
Technical writer
User experience analyst
User experience developer
Video technician
Web developer

Editor's note: The online *Occupational Outlook Handbook* of the US Department of Labor's Bureau of Labor Statistics is an excellent source of information on jobs in hundreds of career fields, including many of those listed here. The *Occupational Outlook Handbook* may be accessed online at www.bls.gov/ooh.

PICTURE CREDITS

ABOUT THE AUTHOR

Terri Dougherty has written dozens of books for young adults and children. She lives in Appleton, Wisconsin, with her husband. They have three grown children who still love playing *Mario Cart* with their cousins at family gatherings. Terri finds the world of video games fascinating. She thanks her nephew for showing her around the world of Twitch and her son for his gaming world connections.